LUFTWAFFE IN COLOUR
FROM GLORY TO DEFEAT 1942–1945

LUFTWAFFE IN COLOUR

From Glory to Defeat 1942–1945

CHRISTOPHE CONY
& JEAN-LOUIS ROBA

CASEMATE | publishers
Philadelphia & Oxford

Published in the United States of America and Great Britain in 2017 by
CASEMATE PUBLISHERS
1950 Lawrence Road, Havertown, PA 19083, USA
and
The Old Music Hall, 106–108 Cowley Road, Oxford OX4 1JE, UK

© Léla Presse
English translation and layout © Casemate Publishers 2017
All photos courtesy of Jean-Louis Roba, unless otherwise stated

Paperback Edition: ISBN 978-1-61200-455-6
Digital Edition: ISBN 978-1-61200-568-3

A CIP record for this book is available from the British Library

Printed and bound in the Czech Republic by FINIDR, s.r.o.

For a complete list of Casemate titles, please contact:

CASEMATE PUBLISHERS (US)
Telephone (610) 853-9131
Fax (610) 853-9146
Email: casemate@casematepublishers.com
www.casematepublishers.com

CASEMATE PUBLISHERS (UK)
Telephone (01865) 241249
Fax (01865) 794449
Email: casemate-uk@casematepublishers.co.uk
www.casematepublishers.co.uk

Errata and Addenda to The Victory Years
Page 45: We can confirm, thanks to Bertrand Hugot, that He 111 P B3+BK (W.Nr. 2497) was shot down by Hurricanes between Épinoy and Oisy-le-Verger, in Pas-de-Calais on May 19th, 1940. Although the K of its code belonged to a second *staffel*, German archives indicate that this was an aircraft of 3./KG 54.
Page 158: The two photographs show Avia B-71 A VG+BQ (W.Nr. 127, built by Aero) of Luftdienstkommando 11, Teil-Kdo 2.11 at Celle, in the winter of 1941–1942

Series design and translation by Hannah McAdams

CONTENTS

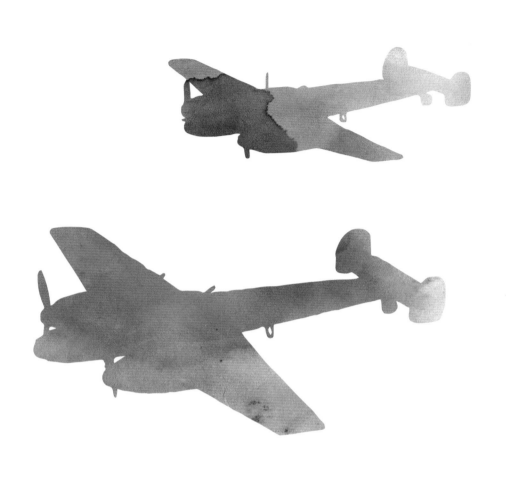

INTRODUCTION

While the Luftwaffe had enjoyed an almost uninterrupted succession of military triumphs from 1939, during the autumn and winter of 1942 its fate changed: the battle of El Alamein and the Allied landings in North Africa sealed its fate on that continent, while its offensive in the USSR – aimed at seizing the oilfields of the Caucasus – ended with the Stalingrad disaster in early 1943. Though the Luftwaffe was a force to be reckoned with during the early years of the Second World War, German aviation was now forced onto the defensive. In the East, the Wehrmacht's last offensive – the battle of Kursk of July–August 1943 – was thwarted by the might of the Soviet forces, which continued to advance towards the Reich. In the south, the Allied landings in Sicily (July 1943) and Italy (September 1943) forced the Germans to withdraw north up the peninsula. To rub salt in the wounds, Mussolini was overthrown, and parts of the Italian army were now taking up arms against their former allies. Finally, in the West, the British and Americans had begun to break the back of their adversary with large, extended air raids, paralyzing Germany's economy and reducing the Luftwaffe's available resources to negligible proportions. On June 6th, 1944 the massive D-Day landings in Normandy commenced, followed by further landings in Provence in the south of France. On June 22nd, on the Eastern Front, the Soviets launched Operation *Bagration* that liberated Belarus in just weeks, and resulted in the occupation of East Prussia and Poland up to the Vistula. It was the beginning of the end for the Luftwaffe. Though it had been the first in the world to use jet engines, therefore ushering in a new era of "modern aviation", the Luftwaffe agonized. It only survived four months after Operation *Bodenplatte*, a futile, last-gasp offensive launched on January 1st, 1945 against the Allied air forces in the West. But its airmen fought on regardless, with a dignified courage that was worthy of their beginnings.

The authors would like to thank everyone who helped them realize this study in colour of the Luftwaffe during the Second World War, especially the Finnish researcher Matti Salonen, without whom this work would never have been completed. Thanks also to Dénes Bernad, Josef Charita, Jean-Marie Gall, Giancarlo Garello, Roberto Gentilli, Bohumir Kudlicka, Michel Ledet, Jacques Moulin, Philippe Ricco, Philippe Saintes, Kari Stenmann, and anyone else whom they might have inadvertently overlooked.

1./JG 1's Bf 109 E-4 (or E-7) "Black 11" at Flushing in the Netherlands, during the winter of 1940–1941. In the second image we can see Sergeant Giuseppe Ruzzin of the 85th Squadron (one of the Corpo Aereo Italiano squadrons that attacked England) posing with Obfw Werner Gerhardt. Note the unusual Plexiglas casing under the fuselage of the Messerschmitt – this houses a Peilgerät IV radio guidance device. *(Roberto Gentilli collection)*

A relaxed atmosphere prior to take-off for this training plane, an Arado Ar 96 painted in two shades of green.

A Ju 88 D-1 from 2. (F)/123 is refuelled by an Opel Kfz 385 tanker in Sicily in the spring of 1941.

Early 1941: Armourers carrying 50kg SC50 bombs in front of a Junkers Ju 87 B-1 on the Channel coast. These photographs are part of the same series found on page 42 of *Luftwaffe in Colour: The Victory Years*. The Stuka seen here belonged to the 2nd squadron (or *staffel*) of an unknown group; we know this from its black and red colouring. The 1st squadron used white, and the 3rd blue.

Above: Saint-Jean-d'Angély, early 1941: This old twin-engined French reconnaissance plane, the Potez 63-11, served as a decoy aircraft for the operations training squadron 2. (Erg.)/JG 53. In the background, armed with four machine guns, is Bf 109 E-8/B (W.Nr. 1237) "15 Black" which was seriously damaged on March 17th, 1941 – just weeks after this photograph was taken – when its engines failed during landing. Despite being approximately 75% damaged, this plane (curiously armed with wing-guns like an E-3) was repaired, upgraded to an E-7 and put back into action at the beginning of 1942 in 2./JG 51 on the Soviet Front. It was then transferred to III./ZG 1 in Africa, where it was lost without a trace after an accident during take-off from Bir el Abd, Egypt, on September 14th, 1942. *(Philippe Ricco collection)*

Opposite, from top:

Hptm Walter Oesau, commander of III./JG 3, photographed on July 12th, 1941 in Polonne, Ukraine, registering seven kills in one day. The bare-headed man wearing sunglasses in the centre is Fw Georg Schentke, who himself claimed five kills that day. Though he was wounded 12 days later when claiming his 86th victim, "Gulle" Oesau figured amongst the great aces of Operation *Barbarossa*, during which he reported 44 victories in less than a month and a half.

This Ar 96 B-1, seen here taking off in Norway, is GA+NH (W.Nr. 960037) of Verbindungstaffel 2. It was severely damaged during a forced landing near Stavanger on October 10th, 1941.

Ju 88 A-4 F1+DD of Stab III./KG 76 in flight over the Soviet Union in early winter 1941. The tips of the propeller cones are painted in the colours of the group's three squadrons: white (7th), red (8th) and yellow (9th). This transport had just been transferred to 9. Staffel (W.Nr. 088 1340), but was damaged by ground fire 30 kilometres north of Moscow on November 30th, 1941.

Two Bf 110 fighter-bombers of 5./SKG 210 preparing to take off on the Eastern Front in early autumn 1941. The wasp symbolizing their squadron (see also *Luftwaffe in Colour: The Victory Years*, pages 93 and 101) has been removed from the noses. These planes are possibly E-2N S9+HN (W.Nr. 4415), which disappeared south of Demidov on February 11th, 1942, and E-1/N S9-IN (W.Nr. 4053), seen next, that went missing south-east of Suchinitschi, near Bryansk on February 28th, 1942 after taking fire in combat. Their squadron became the 5./ZG 1 at that time. *(Roberto Gentilli collection)*

Left: Oblt Max-Hellmuth Ostermann of 3./JG 54 received the Knight's Cross with oak leaves (RK-E) on March 12th, 1942 for his 62nd aerial victory. Ostermann was shot down and killed by an LaGG-3 the following August 9th, with a total of 102 kills.

Below: The vertical tailfin of FW 190 A-2 + − (W.Nr. 20209), flown by Hptm Joachim Müncheberg, commander of II./JG 26, adorned with 67 kill bars, in mid-April 1942. It became "Black 7" of 2./JG 110 training squadron, but was destroyed on November 13th, 1944 near Lautenhain.

Part X

Face-to-Face with the Soviet Steamroller

A mechanic paints a spiral onto the nose cone of a "Friedrich" in early spring 1942. The plane visible in the background – possibly from 2./JG 3 – has been given a yellow engine cowling.

1942 saw the introduction of the first line of an improved version of the Stuka, the Ju 87 D "Dora", equipped with a more powerful and higher-spec Jumo 211 J engine (1,400hp). These Ju 87 D-1s of 7./St.G 1 are flying over the Dnieper region in the summer of 1942, led by J9+AR that has the back of its wheel fairings painted yellow. *(Jacques Moulin collection)*

A Jagdgeschwader 54 Friedrich in flight at sunset.

Left and below: Two views of Bf 109 F-4s of I./JG 3 being overflown by a Fieseler Storch at Rogan, near Kharkov, around June 1942. The terrain is indicative of the vastness of the Ukrainian steppe.

Right: Krasnogwardeisk, June 1942: this I./JG 54 mechanic proudly poses in Bf 109 F-4 <<, which belongs to his commander, Hptm Hans Philipp.

"Fips" Philipp claimed his 100th confirmed kill on June 6th, 1942.

Two Messerschmitt Bf 100s of 7.(H)/LG 2 operating in support of the 6. Armee fly over the countryside near Stalino (Donetsk) in spring 1942.

A 7.(H)/LG pilot 2 consults his logbook while mechanics put the finishing touches to his Bf 110 C-5 L2+MR, which is already equipped with 300-litre drop tanks. The squadron's motif, a magnificent laughing devil, is clearly visible on the nose of the aircraft.

Adolf Hitler visits a muddy airfield, perhaps at Stalino, in the southern sector of the Eastern Front in the spring of 1942. The Führer is seen here next to Heinkel 111 P-2 CA+N (W.Nr. 2741) of his personal squadron, the Fliegerstaffel des Führers. After entering service in October 1938 as D-ADNH, this plane received the *stammkennzeichen* CA+NA in February 1941. It served in the F.d.F. until at least August 1944. The boots in the foreground of the bottom photo are those of an officer who offered them to the Führer so that the latter would not get his own dirty. Hitler politely declined the offer on his arrival, but used them on the return flight, the cabin of a Heinkel He 111 being completely open to the elements.

Above: Bf 109 F-4 "White 8" of I./JG 52 in the Kharkov sector, June 1942. The yellow markings of the Eastern Front have been overlaid with green on the engine cowling and fuselage band.

Below: A Ju 87 B-2 gaining altitude above the Soviet plains in spring 1942. *(Jacques Moulin collection)*

Much farther to the south-west, it was also necessary to maintain an aerial presence, as demonstrated by these three "Emils" in flight near Mizil in late spring 1942. In the foreground E-4 or E-7 "White 6" of the Ölschutzstaffel Ploesti, a Luftwaffe squadron dedicated to the defence of the Romanian oil refineries, is followed by two Bf 109 E-7s of the Romanian Grupul 7 – W.Nr. 1363 "Yellow 65" and W.Nr. 1482 "Yellow 63". It is notable that the Germans and the Romanians used the same bright orange paint for their codes and markings – a far cry from the standard Luftwaffe RLM 04 yellow.

Mechanics struggle to unload this Ju 87 B-1 of 5./St.G 77 based in Ukraine, June–July 1942. The 250kg bomb this plane normally carries has been removed, but it still has four 50kg projectiles attached under its wings.

Three Ju 88 A-4s in formation in the southern sector of the Eastern Front. These bombers come from the 3rd squadron of an unidentified group; unfortunately, most of the markings on these planes have been censored.

A Ju 88 A-4 of Stab III./KG 76 photographed in mid-1942 on the Crimean steppes. The crew of W.Nr. 5757 F1+BD pose here with a one-ton SC 1,000 bomb. The brand-new plane (delivered in April–May 1942) became F1+BR in 7./KG 76. It was 40% damaged when its engine failed on July 2nd outside Kitay, near Sarabouz. Repaired, it was then transferred to 8./KG 1 where it was involved in a minor accident whilst taxiing at Dno on April 17th, 1943. This plane ended its career as a "flying bomb" in 1945 (see story in the final chapter). *(Private collection)*

Above and right: Two shots of Fi 156 C-3 KR+QZ (W.Nr. 5505), which had to land in a field on the Eastern Front in spring 1942 due to engine problems. A passing motorcyclist (riding a captured British BSA M20) stopped to give the mechanic a hand. This Storch appears to have belonged to a medical evacuation unit (*Sanitäts-Flugbereitschaft*), though the insignia that can just be made out on the cowling is very similar to that of I./JG 54.

Below: At the end of spring 1942, a small German naval force was deployed to Lake Ladoga to prevent the Soviets from breaking the Leningrad blockade. To protect its sailors, a detachment of 15 Messerschmitts from 1. and 2./JG 54 arrived in Finland at the beginning of July. Placed under the command of the redoubtable Oblt Hans Götz, who had 33 confirmed kills, they remained there until the beginning of October. This Bf 109 F-4, "Black 7" of Kommando Götz is taking off from Mensuvaara, on the lake's north-western shore, amid swirls of dust, on August 13th. *(SA-kuva)*

The same day, August 13th, 1942, Gen.Ob. Alfred Keller, commander of Luftflotte 1, travelled from Malmi to Mensuvaara on board Heinkel 111 H-6 DL+OC to inspect Kommando Götz. *(SA-kuva)*

Dornier 17 Z-2 A1+BZ of 15.(Kroat)/KG 53 flies over the Ukraine, July 1942.

Beautiful shots of Bf 110 F-2s of 13.(Z)/JG 5 in flight. This squadron of heavy fighters operated in Finland during the summer of 1942. In the foreground is LN+SR, and on its rudder is the first of five kill bars; its usual pilots were either Obfw Karl Munding or Obfw Rudolf Kurpiers, who claimed their fifth kills on May 10th and June 28th, 1942 respectively. Oblt Max Franzisket registered his fifth kill on June 24th, but he is less likely to be the pilot as he scored his sixth victory just four days later. The plane itself (W.Nr. 4568) was lost on February 28th, 1943, its crew having to make a forced landing inside Soviet lines after the plane was damaged in a dogfight. *(Kari Stenmann collection)*

Right: A Ju 87 D-1 or D-3 of 7./St.G 1 warms up its engine in the Dnieper border region during the summer of 1942.

Left: Another view of a Ju 87 D of III./St.G 1 7. Staffel during take-off. This plane has had its wheel casings removed, as they are likely to cause the plane to flip or become unstable on poorly surfaced runways. The motif of the group, a winged helmet on an anchor, recalls the origins of the unit: I./Tr.Gr. 186 was destined to serve on board the *Graf Zeppelin* aircraft carrier but the ship was never completed. *(AVIONS collection)*

Right: A Ju 87 D-1 of 6./St.G 2 escorted by Italian Macchi C.200 fighters of the 21st Gruppo Autonomo C.T. during the Axis advance in the Caucasus, July–August 1942. *(Jacques Moulin collection)*

Generaloberst Richard Ruoff, commander of the 17. Armee, visits the front in a Ju 52 accompanied by General Hiroshi Ōshima. The Japanese general, military attaché to the Japanese ambassador in Berlin, was a competent officer, very interested in new developments in armaments and tactics – hence his frequent visits to the various German fronts.

Left and below: In front of a Soviet hamlet, an officer finishes a conference he has just held with his corps commander next to Fieseler 156 C Storch GF+YF. *(Philippe Ricco collection)*

Right: Pioneers in the field, the Germans developed many types of transport planes, including the Gotha 242 twin boom glider, a copy of the Verbindungskommando (S) 4 – or VK(S) 4 – operating in the summer of 1942 in the southern sector of the Eastern Front. Here ground crew prepare to load drums of fuel

A powered version of the Go 242, the Go 244, was rapidly produced using Gnome-Rhône 14 Ns of French origin. The N1+FQ, photographed in June 1942 at Hagenow just before it departed for the Eastern Front, is a B-1 of the KGrzbV 106, the only group to use this type of plane alongside 1. and 2.(Go)/VK(S) 4.

A fine shot of a Ju 52/3m taxiing somewhere on the Eastern Front. The unit insignia of ??+ZQ cannot be identified, nor can that of the He 111 in the background. The ??+FC code of the Heinkel, however, indicates that it came from the *Stab* (general staff) of a second group.

Major Hannes Trautloft, JG 54 commander, in his new Bf 109 G-2 –+– in September 1942 at Siverskaya. It is clear from this angle that the plane has been fitted with the perfectly vertical back shield plate of a Bf 109 G-1. This variant, with its pressurized cockpit, was never used on the Eastern Front, where most of the dogfighting took place at low and medium altitudes.

Photographed at the end of summer 1942, Obfw Willhelm Schilling plays with fox terrier Chica as he sits in the cockpit of Gf 109 G-2 "Yellow 3" (W.Nr. 10436) that proudly displays the laughing red devil of 9./JG 54 on the engine cowling. This ace claimed his 46th aerial kill on September 12th; four days later, wounded by Soviet flak, he made a forced landing at Doubrovka. W.Nr. 10436 was repaired, but disappeared during a mission on July 25th, 1943 north of Kirkenes whilst serving with Stab II./JG 5. *(Josef Charita collection)*

The rainbow forming behind Bf 109 G-2 of 9./JG 54 is not bringing any good news for the Luftwaffe. On the leading edge of the left wing is an inscription that states it is equipped with wider tyres, with a diameter of 150 × 669mm. This shot was probably taken at Siverskaya at the beginning of autumn 1942.

Stukas of II./St.G 2 return from a mission during autumn 1942. In the foreground is Ju 87 D-1 W.Nr. 2491 T6+DC of the group's general staff, which was shot down by Soviet flak on November 21st, 1942 near Oblivskaya, as the Soviet counter-attack attempted to surround Stalingrad. It had by this time been transferred to 5. Staffel and was designated T6+FN.

Lt Herbert Kuntz (right), one of the best 3./KG 100 pilots (having made his 300th flight of the war on November 11th, 1942), flies Maj Werner Baumbach, commander of III./KG 30 and recipient of the Knight's Cross with oak leaves and swords, in his He 111 H.

A Heinkel 111 H and a Junkers Ju 52/3m during refuelling in the far north, probably Banak, in 1942. The twin-engined plane is likely an H-3 or H-5 of Wetterkette Banak, a detachment of the meteorological reconnaissance squadron Wekusta 5, normally based at Trondheim-Vaernes.

Two Bf 109 G-2s of 6./JG 54 stationed at Rjelbitzi during the winter of 1942–1943. The "Yellow 10" in the foreground is probably W.Nr 13609 that was shot down by an LaGG-3 on January 7th, 1943 north of Ramuschewo, only moments after its pilot, Fw Heinrich Sterr, claimed his 14th kill.

Obfw Maximilian Stotz of 4./JG 54 received the RK-E on October 30th, 1942 after his 100th kill. He claimed a further 82 before falling victim to a Yak-9 on August 19th, 1943.

The Luftwaffe also counted on foreign volunteers like this Spanish pilot, Ramón Escudé-Gisbert, who served on the Eastern Front in 1942 in 15.(Span)/JG 51, also named 2a Escuadrilla Azul. Oblt "Buenooo" Escudé claimed two kills (only one confirmed) before returning to Spain in November 1942.

Major Reinhard Seiler, commander of I./JG 54, registered his 100th kill on July 6th, 1943 during Operation *Citadel*, but he was hit the same day by a Soviet fighter while escorting a Ju 87 south of Orel. Seriously wounded, he never returned to the front.

Major Dr Ernst Kupfer, Kommodore of the Stuka-geschwader 2, welcomes Minister of Equipment Albert Speer to Kertsch on July 2nd, 1943. Two months later Kupfer became commander-in-chief of all ground support units (*General der Schlachtflieger*). He was killed in an accident in Greece on November 6th, 1943.

Oblt Walter Grasemann, Staffelkapitän of 9./KG 27, was awarded the Knight's Cross on October 9th, 1943, eight days after he was promoted to captain. He survived the war with 420 missions under his belt.

The commander of I./Schl.G 1, Hptm Georg Dörffel, was awarded the Knight's Cross with oak leaves on April 14th for having completed over 600 missions. On July 14th, he reached a staggering 800 at Orel.

Mechanics working for Oblt Gerhard Barkhorn, commander of 4./JG 53, work on the glass of the Bf 109 G-2 "White 5" in October 1942. It was in this plane – named Christl after his fiancée – that Barkhorn shot down four LaGG-3 fighters on October 7th, taking his number of kills to 68.

With the arrival of the first snows, BF 109 G-2 –+– of Stab II./ JG 54 receives a coat of white paint made of Ikarin-A2515.21, a sort of paste that can be diluted with artificial resin. Like Kommodore Trautloft's aircraft, this "Gustav" is equipped with the vertical shield panel of a Bf 109 G-1.

One of the last Junkers 87 B-2 still in service on the front lines of the Eastern Front during winter 1942–1943. The Doras had by then totally replaced the Berthas and Richards. *(PK)*

Mechanics work on an He 111 Z in the USSR. This was a combination of two He 111 H-6 bombers, to which a fifth Jumo 221 F engine was added. The twin-fuselage "Zwilling" was conceived to pull the gigantic Me 321 gliders for long distances. Only 15 of these strange planes were ever made before a motorized version of the Me 321 – the Me 323 – entered service.

Two shots of Fw 190 A-4/U3s and A-5/U3s of 6./Sch.G. 1 lined up in early 1943 on the tarmac at the Deblin–Irena base in Poland, where this squadron had previously been using Bf 109 Es. When the Germans made advances on the Eastern Front in March, the colours of the individual codes were repainted in black so they wouldn't be confused with Soviet planes. *(Signal)*

Top: This photograph was reputedly taken during the winter of 1942–1943 on the Eastern Front. If so this Ju 87 B-2 would have belonged to 9./St.G 77, therefore its code would be S2+BT. *(PK)*

Above: An excellent shot of an He 111 H-6 of 8./KG 53 about to land in Dno, on the north-east of the Soviet Front. The plane is armed with an MG FF 20mm nose cannon and an MG 15 7.92mm machine gun. The A1+BS (W.Nr. 7799) was damaged by ground fire on January 5th, 1943 south-east of Velikiye Luki.

Top: The 1.(F)/124 also used twin-engined Junkers, like this Ju 88 D-1 photographed taxiing at Kirkenes-Høybuktmoen on June 20th, 1943. The squadron used this as a base for surveillance of the port at Murmansk, where Allied convoys docked to resupply the USSR. *(Philippe Ricco collection)*

Above: Luftwaffe officers in Nikolskoye Street, Smolensk in early 1943. The town was liberated by the Red Army the following September 25th.

The pilot of < of Stab I./JG 54 scrambles, spring 1943. His FW 190 A-4 has a 500kg bomb under its fuselage.

Opposite, from top:

Jagdgeschwader 54 started exchanging its Messerschmitt Bf 109s for Focke-Wulfs during the winter of 1942–1943. This photo, taken in early 1943, shows FW 190 A-4 "White 9" that belonged to Uffz Karl Schnörrer of 1./JG 54. The plane still wears its winter whitewash.

The DFS 230 and Gotha 242 gliders still had very limited carrying capacity. In 1940, to solve this problem, the Messerschmitt firm devised a new glider that was so big it could carry a Panzer II tank: the Me 321 Gigant. It was used on the Eastern Front for the first time in early 1943. Seen here is an example of the Me 321 Gigant; the plane overflying in the distance is an Fi 156 Storch.

In mid-February 1943, two weeks after Stalingrad fell to the Soviets, this giant Me 321 B glider from the Grossraumlastensegler-Kommando 2 (G.S. Kdo 2) transported reinforcements to the bridgehead that the Germans were holding at Kouban. W6+SW was photographed at Slavyanskaya alongside its tow-plane – the He 111 Z TM+K1, at the far right of the image – and two Bf 109 G-2s from the JG 52. On the left is "White 3" (W.Nr. 19310) of 4./JG 52, which was later lost when its engine failed south of Anapa on March 20th. To the right of the Me 321 B is –+– (W.Nr. 14856) that belonged to Geschwaderkommodore Major Dietrich Hrabak, which was 70% destroyed on March 30th during a forced landing east of Dniepropetrovsk.

A Messerschmitt Bf 109 G-4/R3 of 1.(F)/124 in flight over the Kirkenes region in the far north of Norway at the end of May 1943. This single-seater reconnaissance plane, equipped with a camera, was fresh from the factory and had not yet been assigned a code. Its pilot was Oblt Willi Lerch, who was later transferred to 1.(F)/120 based at Stavanger-Sola, on the south-western tip of Norway. He disappeared at sea on November 17th following an attempt to photograph the raid at Scapa Flow.

Three Focke-Wulf 189 A-2s of 7.(H)/32, armed with 50kg underwing bombs, in flight over the USSR in the spring of 1943. The symbol of the tactical reconnaissance squadron, a red 7 on a white shield, is painted on the engine cowlings. In the foreground is M4+IR (W.Nr. 125141) that was damaged by a Soviet fighter plane on May 28th, south of Kiewskoje, injuring its crew of three. At rear is M4+ER (W.Nr. 2256) that disappeared after being rammed by an enemy plane on August 7th, 1943, four kilometres north of Kiewskoje, killing its crew.

Above: A superb view of a flight of FW 190 A-5s from 1./JG 54 "free hunting" in the central sector of the Eastern Front in the summer of 1943. Like the bottom two photos on page 39, the superior camouflage of these planes is composed of three tones: dark green, dark brown and black.

Above: Three FW 190 A-5s of 5./JG 54 being serviced near Orel in July 1943. In the foreground, the "Black 5" is that of Oblt "Max" Stotz, who disappeared in another plane on August 19th near Vitebsk after dogfight with a Yak-9. He had registered 182 aerial victories. Behind "Black 5" is "Black 7", which belonged to Lt Emil Lang, and "Black 6", which, like the former, has its engine cowling painted orange.

Below: The same planes viewed from another angle on a separate occasion. The photo shows that these are indeed A-5s rather than A-6s, which they are often mistakenly identified as. The armaments of the two versions are different: an MG FF/M short-barrelled cannon and an MG 151/20 long-barrelled cannon on each wing of the A-5, and two MG 151/20s on each wing of the A-6.

Above: The wrecks of two Focke-Wulf 190 fighters photographed on the border of the Kharkov sector in July 1943. "White F" in the foreground appears to have belonged to 1./Schl.G 1, while FW 190 A-5/ US <A+– behind it probably came from Stab II./Schl.G 1.

Above: Bf 109 G-6 "White 10" (W.Nr. 15591) of 1./JG 52 is serviced at Kuteinikowo in July 1943. On July 28th, having taken fire in a dogfight, this plane was on fire when it crash-landed.

Right: Oblt Walter Grasemann listens to a report from one of his subordinates at the end of summer in 1943. The Heinkel 111 1G+BT behind them being refuelled is H-16/R1 W.Nr. 8479, which fell victim to a Soviet fighter near Woroschilowka on the following September 29th. This version was the first to benefit from a DL 131 dorsal turret powered by an electronic motor and armed with an MG 131 13mm machine gun.

Above left: As a huge consumer of men and materials, the Eastern Front required constant shipments of reinforcements. It was in this context that IV./JG 54 was formed in July 1943; the squadron was in the USSR a month later. Seen here undergoing maintenance at Siverskaya is Bf 109 G-6 "White 1" (W.Nr. 15986) of 10. Staffel that was lost in combat on September 3rd along with its pilot, Uffz Karl-Heinz Leitner.

Above right: Combat raged in the far north too, as shown in this photograph taken in Petsamo, Finland, in August 1943. Oblt Theodor Weissenberger, Staffelkapitän of 7./JG 5, points to the decoration that has just been painted onto the tailfin of his Bf 109 G-2. The ace had recently been awarded the Knight's Cross with oak leaves for his 108th–112th kills, on July 25th.

Left: Obfw Helmut Benkendorff, 5./St.G 1 pilot, passes in front of Ju 88 D-5 A5+MN in August 1943. He carries a bunch of flowers given to him by his comrades on the occasion of his 500th mission. Awarded the Knight's Cross in March 1944, "Mukki" Benkendorff survived the war with 666 combat missions and 12 aerial victories to his name, an unusually high "score" for a Stuka pilot.

These four shots taken in the Ukraine at the end of summer in 1943 – at Kharkov or Lvov, according to different sources – show a team of mechanics working on the left half-axle of a Gigant that had suffered from a shaky landing. The repairs made to this Me 323, named Himmelslaus, are clearly visible thanks to the application of a red protective coat.

Left: This amazing Storch variation is an Fi 156 E-0, identical to the C-1 except for the twin wheels on each of its legs, installed to aid landing and take-off on uneven ground. Only ten pre-production planes were ever built.

The staff of a flak unit, recognizable from their bright red collar tags, participate in the construction of a building in the Varsovie sector. On the left is a *hauptwachtmeister* (chief warrant officer), and center is a *major* (commandant).

Hans-Joachim Jäschke, Staffel-führer of 4./SG 1, receives the Knight's Cross on March 26th, 1944. He was hit by Soviet flak on the following July 21st after destroying 78 tanks and completing 550 missions.

Obstlt Dietrich Hrabak, Kommodore of JG 52, was awarded the RK-E on November 25th, 1943 in recognition of his 118 aerial victories. He ended the war as the head of JG 54.

On October 14th, 1943, Hptm Walter Nowotny, commander of I./JG 54 became the first pilot in history to achieve 250 kills. He was awarded the Knight's Cross of the Iron Cross with oak leaves, swords and diamonds a month later. He didn't return to the front until the summer of 1944, whereupon he commanded an Me 262 jet fighter test unit. Nowotny was killed returning from a mission on the following November 8th.

Commander of I./JG 54, Major Horst Ademeit, disappeared in combat on August 8th, 1944 in southern Latvia. He had 166 kills to his name.

In the spring of 1944, the most celebrated ace in the Luftwaffe was Major Gerhard Barkhorn, commander of II./JG 52, who registered his 273rd victory on May 31st in Romania. Gravely wounded the same day by a Soviet P-39, he returned to the front five months later and ended the war with 301 aerial victories.

Obfw Herbert Hampe, a Ju 88A pilot from II./KG 3, photo-graphed after being awarded the Knight's Cross in April 1944.

Two crew members of a Ju 88 A-4 on the steppes. In early 1944 the twin-engined Junkers were relocated from the Eastern Front to the Western and Mediterranean fronts where they would be less vulnerable than the "old" He 111s.

A shot of two Junkers Ju 87 D-5s in flight over the Eastern Front. This Stuka variation, characterized by its elongated wings and two MG 151 20mm cannons, entered service in July 1943.

A Flakvierling 38 (a quadruple 20mm anti-aircraft gun) in action on the Eastern Front. After 1943, the Luftwaffe was no longer able to contain the Soviet air force, so ground troops were often entrusted with keeping them at bay using flak.

Above: Two He 111 H-16s, painted in a very unusual camouflage, in Hungary in the spring of 1944. These planes possibly belong to the Kampfgeschwader 4 "General Wever", who used this type of bomber until the end of the war.

Below: Two views of Ju 87 D-5s of II./SG 1 taken at the beginning of April 1944 in snow-covered Rovaniemi, near the Arctic Circle, where the group attacked the railway serving the port of Murmansk, where British supplies were being delivered.

Sometimes the Luftwaffe had to share their airfields with cows: this bucolic scene has as its subject Me 323 E-1 C8+RP of 6./TG 5 and was taken in May 1943 at Ianca in the south-east of Romania.

Above: Ground staff unload equipment from a Ju 52/3m, the "servant" of the Luftwaffe transport units.

Below: This medical evacuation Ju 52/3m, photographed behind three graves, is symbolic of how the Germans saw the Eastern Front in the summer of 1944: a chasm into which German troops disappeared bit by bit. *(Private collection)*

Part XI
The Mediterranean Front

Above: Bf 110s of Zerstörergeschwader 26 "Horst Wessel" at Trapani, Sicily, in front of Mount St. Giullano. *(Jacques Moulin collection)*

Below: This postcard shows Ju 88 D-2 4U+EK (W.Nr. 880805) of 2.(F)/123 at Kastelli, Crete, in the spring of 1942. Under its wing, the aircraft carries a 900-litre drop tank necessary for its long-distance reconnaissance missions over the Mediterranean. First 35% damaged when its one engine failed on take-off on March 22nd, 1942 in Athens, this Junkers was 95% destroyed on the following November 23rd during an enemy bombing raid on Kastelli.

Two Messerschmitt Bf 110 E-2s from 8./ZG 26 approach the Sicilian coast after crossing the Mediterranean. Behind 3U+KS (clumsily doctored by a censor in the second shot) is SB+GO (W.Nr. 4419), which crashed at Derna, Libya on May 26th, 1942 after being hit by anti-aircraft fire.

Lt "Rudi" Sinner, technical officer of I./JG 27, poses with two mechanics on his Bf 109 F-4 <T during spring 1942. After becoming Staffelkapitän of 6./JG 27, this talented Austrian pilot had claimed 31 kills by the following September.

An "Auntie Ju" has its tyres changed at its North African base in 1942.

Two of Stab I./St.G 3's planes in Libya. On the left is a Dornier 17 Z, and on the right Caudron C.445 Goéland no. 9303/567 DF+UO that was 25% damaged on May 19th, 1942 during a forced landing at Derna. *(Philippe Ricco collection)*

Ju 52/3ms fly over Tripoli in 1942. The H in the foreground has a small white 8 on its tailfin.

A Friedrich returning from a mission raises a cloud of sand as it taxies. This front-on view allows us to clearly see the tropical air filter on the side on its engine cowling.

Above: Oblt Hans-Joachim Marseille, the new Staffelkapitän of 3./JG 27, is congratulated by his wingman, Fw Rainer Pöttgen, on his return from a successful mission in June 1942. His plane is Bf 109 F-4 "Yellow 14" (W.Nr. 10137), which was destroyed on the following July 25th during an enemy bombing raid on Turbiya, near El Daba in Egypt.

Above: Marseille photographed on June 28th, 1942, the date Adolf Hitler awarded him the Knight's Cross with oak leaves and swords in recognition of his 101 aerial victories.

Below: Ju 87 D-1 S7+EP (W.Nr. 2530) of 6./St.G. 3 in flight over the African coast at the end of spring 1942. This Stuka, which still has its European camouflage, was hit by a British fighter on June 26th, 1942 at Mersa Matruh.

Mechanics changing an engine on Bf 109 F-4 <+– of Stab II./JG 27, a plane regularly piloted by Oblt Otto Schulz. This other great ace of JG 27 (51 kills) was hit on June 17th, 1942 near Sidi Rezegh by a Curtiss P-40 Kittyhawk of 260 Squadron RAF.

While life in the desert wasn't always easy, the men of JG 27 and their Italian colleagues were occasionally treated to a performance, like this magic show. In the centre, with his head tilted back, is Lt Werner Schroer of Stab I./JG 27. In the left foreground, wearing dark sunglasses, is the "Star of Africa", Oblt Hans-Joachim Marseille (3./JG 27).

Although present in great numbers on the Eastern Front, the FW 189 was a rare sight in the African skies, as only one *staffel* – 1.(H)/Aufkl.Gr 23 – was deployed during the summer of 1942. 6K+KN was photographed at this time in Libya.

Fi 156 C-3 PP+QL (W.Nr. 5451) from the Flugbereitschaft of the Fliegerführer Afrika in 1942. This Storch wears wholly "sand" camouflage, but hasn't yet received the white markings of the Mediterranean Front.

Right: Jagdgeschwadwer 27 catch up on their laundry.

Below: A bird's-eye view of an aerodrome in North Africa, where Luftwaffe planes stand alongside those of the Regia Aeronautica.

He 111 H-6 LT 1H+GN of 5./KG 26 landing at Catania, in the south-east of Sicily, in mid-1942. This special variant of the Heinkel 111, which carries two 765kg LT F5b torpedoes under its belly, was used for night attacks on convoys in the Mediterranean.

A superb shot of Ar 196 A-2 7R+BK of 2./SAG 125 being serviced at the Cretan port of Souda in September 1942. The unit was experiencing serious maintenance problems at this time.

Right: Ar 196 A–2
7R+KK being inspected by
mechanics in 1942.

Left: Dornier 24 N-1
W.Nr. 008 KK+UM
– the last part of its
code has unfortunately
been censored – of 6./
Seenotstaffel anchored at
Syracuse in mid-1942.
The crew of this squadron
operated between Sicily
and Malta to recover
ships wrecked in the
Mediterranean. This plane
was accidently destroyed in
the attack on Messina the
following November 14th.

Right: A Do 24 T from
7./Seenotstaffel seen in the
Mediterranean in 1942.
This version differs from
the Do 24 N due to its
Bramo 323 R-2 engines
and deeper cowling.

Albert Kesselring, commander-in-chief of the Mediterranean Front, visits Luftwaffe units in Africa. The Generalfeldmarschall flew himself to visit the airmen in his own Dornier 215 B, which we can see retains the green-toned camouflage from when it was based in Italy.

Above: Mechanics work on the engines of a Ju 88 A-4 of 2./KG 54 "Totenkopf" in Gerbini, Sicily, while attacks were being carried out against Malta in the summer of 1942. B3+EK (W.Nr. 0885898) was hit on September 2nd off the coast of Benghazi.

Below: Ju 52/3m 4F+KE of the KGrzb V 400 flying from Trapani to Tunis in November 1942, at the time Allied troops were landing in North Africa. The three-engined plane has tactical code P4 K painted in yellow on its tailfin.

Left: Generalfeldmarschall Erwin Rommel, commander-in-chief of the Deutsche Afrika Korps, inspects a heavy flak unit in Africa. The "Desert Fox", very close to his troops, visited them often, and was frequently found crossing the front at the controls of a Fieseler Storch.

Above: A Flak 18 88mm anti-aircraft gun protecting an airfield in the Libyan Desert. This extremely efficient weapon was also used in a ground role against tanks.

Right: Oblt Franz Götz, Staffelkapitän of 9./JG 53, received the Knight's Cross on September 4th, 1942. He had registered 40 aerial victories at that time.

Far right: Generalleutnant Otto Hoffmann von Waldau, commander-in-chief of German aviation in Africa, photographed during the summer of 1942. He is wearing the Knight's Cross awarded the previous June.

Various views of a Friedrich undergoing maintenance in the desert. While one mechanic paints the JG 27 insignia on the engine cowling, others supply the armaments.

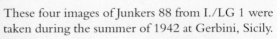

These four images of Junkers 88 from I./LG 1 were taken during the summer of 1942 at Gerbini, Sicily.

Opposite – clockwise, from top left:

A 2./LG 1 pilot wearing a white summer cap poses in front of his plane, which has red-tierced propeller cones; Hptm Joachim Helbig, commander of I./LG 1, wears the Knight's Cross with oak leaves he received on January 16th, 1942. Very active in Erwin Rommel's summer offensives, "Jochen" Helbig added swords to his decoration in recognition for sinking 182,000 tons of enemy shipping in 330 combat missions; This sand-coloured Ju 88 A-4 from 2./LG 1 has the Lehrgeschwader 1 emblem on its nose: a rampant red Pomeranian griffin on a white coat of arms; Due to a lack of underground ammunition bunkers, I./LG 1 kept these one-ton SC 1,000 bombs under armed guard in the open.

Below: Two views of Ju 52/3m North Africa–Europe shuttle aircraft.

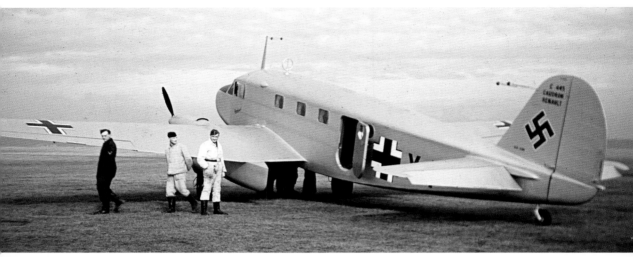

Top: Caudron C.445 Goéland no. 9217/481 CD+YF served as a shuttle plane for the general staff of Luftflotte 2 in Italy.

Above: The enormous BV 222 V-5 X4+EH of the Lufttransportstaffel (See) 222 in the Cretan port of Heraklion at the end of 1942. Note the large loading door and code S5 on the rudder. Adapted for marine reconnaissance and assigned to the Fliegerführer Atlantik, this six-engined seaplane was destroyed by de Havilland Mosquitoes of 264 Squadron at Biscarrosse on June 20th, 1943.

Left: Major Heinz Bär, photographed in early April 1943, while commanding I./JG 77 in Tunisia. By this time, he had accumulated 175 kills from across the various fronts.

Top: In early 1942, aware that its Ju 52/3ms didn't have the necessary capacity to effectively resupply the Deutsche Afrika Korps, Germany acquired several three-engined Savoia S.82s from its Italian allies and with them formed a Savoiastaffel in III./KGzbV 1. This S.82 1Z+ED (W.Nr. 134), photographed at the beginning of 1943 at Lecce, has the squadron motif on its cockpit – a bear between two crossed palms. On the tailfin is tactical code Z5E. *(Giancarlo Garello collection)*

Above: Late March 1943, a convoy of RAF trucks at Gabès air base that has just been captured by the Allies. In the foreground is Ju 52/3m C3+OH of the Tr.St./II.Fl.Korps, which appears to have been scuttled by the retreating German troops.

Right: FW 190 A pilots of II./JG 2 in Tunisia, early 1943. Third from the left is Oblt Erich Rudorffer (commander of 6. Staffel), who shot down his 49th adversary on the morning of January 8th. By March 12th, he had 73 kills to his name.

Me 323 D-6 RF+XD (W.Nr. 1130), a 1st group plane in the Kampfgeschwader zur besonderen Verwendung 323 (I./KG.zbV. 323), seen some time before it crash-landed at Castelvetrano on March 30th, 1943.

This P-38 Lightning, shot down during the campaign in Tunisia (December 1942–January 1943), has the code ES-J, which shows it belonged to 48. FS/14. FG. This photograph was published by *Signal* magazine in May 1943. *(Signal)*

It's all over for the Germans in Africa. An American soldier climbs onto the wing of Henschel 129 B "Red C" (W.Nr. 0432) of 8.(Pz)/Sch.G 2, abandoned at the side of El Aouina airfield in Tunis, May 1943.

Taken at Casa Zeperra, in the south of Sardinia after an air raid in June/July 1943, this photograph shows the wreckage of two Bf 109 G-6s of II./JG 51. In the foreground is "Yellow 17" of 4. Staffel; behind it, on fire, is "Black 6" of 5. Staffel.

Being towed by a tractor is Arado 196 A–3 6W+KK of 2./SAG 128, a squadron based in the south of France in 1943.

Crete 1943: an armorer brings a now redundant 50kg bomb from Ar 196 of 2./SAG 125 to dry land after an uneventful mission.

After conquering North Africa in May 1943, the Allies were ready to open a second front in Europe, commencing with Operation *Husky* on July 10th, the landings in Sicily. This German Marder II tank is being loaded onto an Me 323 D-6 Gigant of I./TG 5 during reinforcement operations to the island. C8+AB (W.Nr. 1142, code X1 C on the tailfin) suffered 50% damage on landing at Pistoia, near Florence, on July 21st, 1943.

This little Gotha 145 C3+VH, the shuttle plane for Transportstaffel/II. Fliegerkorps, is seen here in Sicily in the company of a three-engined Ju 52/3m from 10./KGzbV 1.

This French aircraft LeO 451T DK+ZD, from the manufacturers Lioré and Olivier, was used as a transport plane by the Luftwaffe before being captured in Sicily during the summer of 1943. For a while it served with the 57th Fighter Group USAAF.

Above left: When the Americans set their minds to repainting a plane, there was nothing subtle about the outcome! This Fw 190 A-4, retrieved from Gerbini in July 1943 by members of 85th Fighter Squadron, 79th Fighter Wing, is now entirely red and yellow. Pilots of the "Flying Skulls" (a glimpse of their insignia is just visible on the cockpit) were able to take a few flights in it before it was transferred to the Constantine Fighter Training Center. *(Philippe Ricco collection)*

Above right: Another example of a German plane with American markings, this Bf 109 G-2/R2 (W.Nr. 10605) named Irmgard was previously "Black 14" of 2.(H)/14. Forced to belly-land in Tunisia by British infantrymen, this reconnaissance Gustav was, the following month, offered to the airmen of 87th Fighter Squadron, 79th Fighter Wing, who restored it to flight condition and were eager to repaint it in their colours. It was transferred to the testing facility at Wright Field and was scrapped the following year.

A Junkers 87 R–3 of II./LLG 1 towing a glider (out of frame) in the Aix–les–Milles region of France in the summer of 1943.

Above and below: Two shots of Bf 109 G-6 "Yellow 1" of Lt Alfred Hammer, Staffelkapitän of 6./JG 53, taken in early August 1943 at Cancello, Italy, around 30km north-west of Naples. The man shaving in the second picture is Fw Eugen Kurz.

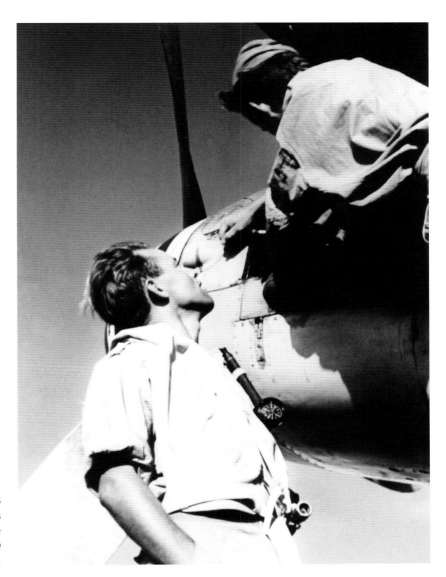

Fw Kurz watches one of his mechanics working on the cowling of a Bf 109 G-6 at Cancello.

Ju 52/3m 4U+NH served as a shuttle for 1.(F)/123 reconnaissance squadron based in Parma, in the north of Italy, from 1943 to 1944.

In early September 1943, the Allied invasion of Italy was underway. This magnificent Bf 110 G-2 of 6./ ZG1 was captured on the 9th of the month at the Montecorvino Rovella base, south-east of Salerno. Having arrived on the Eastern Front in April of the same year, the second group of the famous Wasps suffered several destructive bombing raids during July and had to leave many of their planes behind when they were transferred to Brittany at the beginning of August. S9+AP is one of those, probably W.Nr. 6250, which was 25% damaged on July 13th. Behind it is an Fw 190 A-5/U8 of III./SKG 10 and three training biplanes of the Regia Aeronautica, which wear the identification markings of the Foligno flight school south-east of Perugia.

This Focke-Wulf 190 G-3 was also photographed at Montecorvino Rovella in September 1943. Bearing the factory code DN+FV, W.Nr. 160022 was abandoned on the 9th of the month by retreating German troops just after it was acquired by 10./SKG 10. The American airmen of the 31st Fighter Group succeeding in repairing it a few days later, but they got little use out of it: during a test flight, one was on the verge of being shot down by a group of A-36 Invaders – the assault version of the P-51 Mustang.

When Benito Mussolini was incarcerated in Gran Sasso in central Italy following the overthrow of his government on July 25th, 1943, Hitler ordered SS Hauptsturmführer Otto Skorzeny, a specialist in "delicate" missions, to help Mussolini escape. This resulted in Operation *Eiche* on September 12th, 1943. Twelve DFS 230 gliders landed on the tiny plateau at the foot of the Campo Imperatore, 2,100 metres above sea level. Benefitting from the total confusion in the Italian Carabinieri, 90 paratroopers assisted by 16 Waffen-SS were able to liberate the Duce, who was exfiltrated thanks to Fi 156 C-3 SJ+LL (W.Nr. 1268) piloted by Hptm Heinrich Gerlach of the Transportstaffel/XI. Fliegerkorps. The first shot shows Mussolini climbing aboard a Storch, aided by Gerlach; Skorzeny is already on board. In the second photo, Mussolini's large rotund silhouette is visible in the back of the departing plane, as the men of the 1st Battalion, Fallschirmjäger-Regiment 7 wave him off. The pilot narrowly avoided disaster when the plane had one of its landing-gear wheels torn off by a rock, sending the plane careering off into the void. After a terrifying nosedive, Gerlach – formerly General Kurt Student's personal pilot – used his skill and resourcefulness to pull up just metres from the valley floor, landing in Avezzano despite the damage it had suffered. Heinrich Gerlach received the Knight's Cross for his efforts, as did Skorzeny and the glider pilots who took part in the mission.

Above: An anti-aircraft spotlight (*scheinwerfer*) being used by a flak battery in Italy.

Below: Ar 196 A-3s of 4./SAG 126 in Souda Bay, Crete, await their next mission.

Above: Lt Ernst-Wilhelm Reinert, Staffelkapitän of 3./JG 77, on the cover of *Die Wehrmacht* magazine, October 27th, 1943. He had 167 confirmed kills to his name at the time. During the four months of the Tunisian campaign alone, this exceptional pilot registered 52 kills. *(Die Wehrmacht)*

Above: Bf 109 G-6/R6 "White 9" of 7./JG 27 landed on its nose towards the end of 1943, probably at Maleme in Crete. This *kanonenboot*, or gunship, armed with 20mm cannons under its wings, was piloted by Uffz Rudolf "Pongo" Moycis during the month of December.

Below: An Arado 196 A-3 takes off in Crete in 1944, in front of another plane from 4./SAG 126 (ex 2./SAG 125). The undersides of the engine cowlings are painted yellow.

The "ambulance" version of the Storch was the Fi 156 D-1, characterized by the addition of a small triangular window behind the canopy and an expanded loading door on the left side. This D-1 with the factory code GF+KI comes from the Sanitäts-Flugbereichschaft 7 stationed at Kalamaki, Greece in 1943–1944.

Right: A Ju 188 D-1 captured at Florence airport at the end of July 1944, with Spitfire LF VIII s/no. MT800 of 154 Squadron RAF in the background. This reconnaissance version is characterized by its Junkers Jumo 213 in-line motors, as opposed to the F-1's BMW 801 radial engines.

Left: A close-up of the upper rear turret of a Ju 188 F-1 on the Mediterranean Front, perhaps of 3.(F)/33, in 1944. Designated LLG 131, this type of glass turret was armed with an MG 131 13mm machine gun.

Part XII

The West:
From One Landing
to the Next

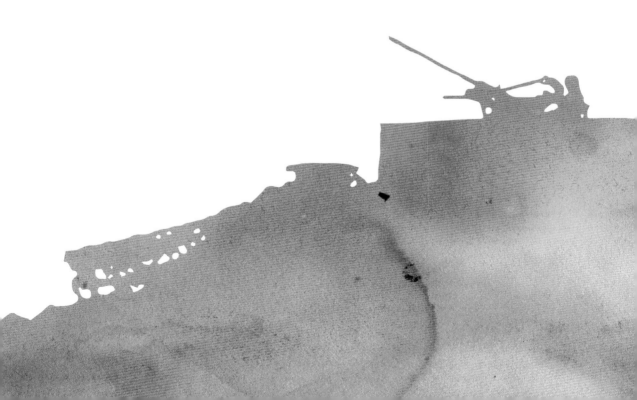

One of two Focke-Wulf 200 C-4/U2s of the Fliegerstaffel des Führers, Hitler's air transport squadron, seen on the slopes of Ainring near Salzburg. It is probably CE+IC (W.Nr. 0138), the second C-4/U2 produced being Admiral Dönitz's GC+SJ (W.Nr. 0181) Albatros III. The F.d.F. used 40 of these planes during the war, 13 of which were different versions of the FW 200 Kondor.

Below left: Former glider pilot turned JG 54 fighter pilot, Hptm Wolfgang Späte (79 kills) was named commander of the Erprobungskommando 16 in May 1942, charged with developing the Me 163 Komet rocket-powered fighter.

Below right: Späte called on his squadron comrade Oblt Josef Pöhs (43 kills) to second him in the Erpr.Kdo 16, but he was killed on December 30th, 1943 while testing a non-motorized version of the Me 163.

The following series of photographs was taken at Bordeaux–Mérignac, probably at the beginning of March 1942, a little before 1. and 3./KG 40 were posted to the Norwegian base of Trondheim-Vaernes, to track Allied convoys operating in the Arctic.

Above: An FW 200 C-3 or C-4 Kondor returns from a mission with a feathered outer starboard propeller.

Right: The crew chat with their squadron colleagues, who have come to welcome them back from their mission.

Upper left: The pilot smokes a well-deserved cigarette after a 15-hour flight.

Centre left: Derived from a four-engined Lufthansa plane, the Kondor could also serve as a transport for a range of equipment, as seen in this image.

Below left: I./KG 40 personnel in discussion at Bordeaux-Mérignac in front of Ju 52/3mg5e TE+DQ (W.Nr. 6977). Although it has the Red Cross markings, this three-engined Sanitäts–Flugbereichschaft 7 plane was nonetheless shot down by an Allied fighter on January 7th, 1943 during a flight from Tunis to Trapani.

Below right: Hptm Edmund Daser, commander of I./KG 40, wears the Knight's Cross he was awarded on February 21st, 1941 for having personally sunk 58,000 tons of enemy shipping.

Perched on the windscreen of a Friedrich in February/March 1942, this Obfw pilot of I./JG 3 is being helped into his parachute harness by a mechanic before setting off on a training flight from Wiesbaden-Erbenheim. This photograph was featured in *Die Wehrmacht* magazine on May 27th, 1942. *(Die Wehrmacht)*

In this photograph, taken moments later, we can see more of the plane: a Bf 109 F-1 or F-2, as indicated by its C3 octane rating. Several old Bf 109 E-7s, F-1s and F-2s from the Ergänzunggruppe JG 53 were used to train pilots of I./JG 3 before this group returned to the Eastern Front at the end of April 1942, equipped entirely with Bf 109 F-4s. *(Die Wehrmacht)*

Below: An anti-aircraft artillery position on the English Channel. The gun is a 20mm Flak 38.

This report, which appeared in *Signal*, shows the pilot of FW 190 A "Yellow 8" preparing to depart for a mission over the English Channel in 1942. *(Signal)*

Clockwise, from left: A mechanic helps the pilot into his inflatable life vest, designated Luftschwimmweste Fl. 30154.

Attached to his wrist, an AK39 Fl. 23235 compass produced by Kladec of Prague.

The pilot has eight Erkennungssignal cartridges in the front left pocket of his pants, which he can use to signal for help in the case of a forced landing at sea. These can be fired from the pistol he holds in his right hand.

Another essential survival item: a 100g box of Scho-Ka-Kola caffeinated chocolate.

With his oxygen mask already fixed in place, the Focke-Wulf pilot poses for the photographer one last time before taking off.

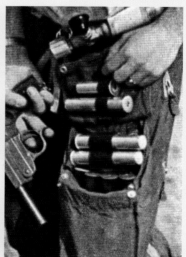

Above: Contrary to what this propaganda shot of a Bf 109 F night fighter with 18 kill bars on its tailfin would suggest, this Friedrich never served in this role in a regular Luftwaffe unit. It wasn't until spring 1943 that an FW 190 A and Bf 109 G Nachtjagdversuchskommando (NJVK) was created; this was the predecessor of the "Wilde Sau" single-seater night-fighter units. *(Signal)*

Right: Initially, the Nachtjagd (Night Fighters) had to carry out its missions in Bf 110s, Ju 88s and Do 215/217s. But it was on board a Grunau "Baby" IIb glider that Hptm Werner Streib, commander of I./NJG 1, trained as much as he was able from the Dutch base of Venlo. This ace had 25 night kills by May 1942.

The most important development of the Do 17 resulted in the Dornier 217 E bomber, which entered service at the end of 1941 in Kampfgeschwader 2 of II./KG 40. It was initially limited to the European Front, but made a critical impression during Operation *Jubilee*: the attempted British landing at Dieppe on August 9th, 1942 resulted in bitter failure for the assailants. *(PK)*

The upper gunner of a Do 217 E in his DL 131 turret, armed with a heavy MG 131 13mm machine gun.

On September 24th, 1942, Oblt Walter Bornschein (Staffelkapitän of 4./KG 2) received the Knight's Cross for his squadron's performance during the Dieppe operation.

In September 1942, III./JG 26 received several important visitors to its Belgian base at Wevelghem. One of these was Professor Kurt Tank, chief engineer of Focke-Wulf, seen here with the commander of the gruppe, Hptm Josef Priller (left).

Tank was accompanied by the person responsible for the FW 190 programme, Chief Engineer Rudolf Blaser, who is shown here having climbed onto the wing of FW 190 A-2 <+I (W.Nr. 20206) to hear the thoughts of Fw Walter Grünlinger, who has just returned from a mission. Priller's wingman flies his commander's old FW, Jutta, renamed Rata, which is visible on the seven of hearts painted under the windshield.

The Kommandeur of III./JG 26 is introduced to the engineer "Willy" Messerschmitt, the founder of the Messerschmitt company. "Pips" Priller had just returned from a flight in his new FW 190 A-3 <<+I (W.Nr. 0552), decorated with 77 kill bars.

"White 14" is an FW 190 A-2 or A-3 of 1./JG 2 based at Triqueville, 30km east of Le Havre, at the end of 1942.

This He 177 A-1 is probably VE+UO of Erprobungsstaffel 177, which was in an accident on December 21st, 1942. The ESt. 177 was charged with refining the operational version of the curious heavy bomber developed by Heinkel, a "real-fake" four-engined plane, as it was equipped with two DB 606 of 2,700hp, which are actually just two pairings of two DB 601s.

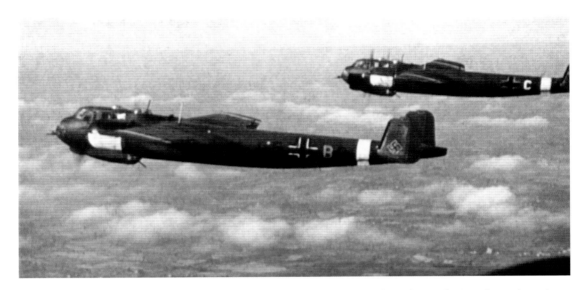

Two Do 217 E-4s of Stab III./KG 2 in flight between Bordeaux and Toulouse during Operation *Anton* in November 1942. All Luftwaffe planes that participated in the occupation of the southern theatre had white bands at the end of the fuselage before the tailplane. Transferred to 7./KG 2, W.Nr. 4237 U5+BD in the foreground was shot down by a Bristol Beaufighter night fighter of 219 Squadron on March 12th/13th, 1943 near the mouth of the Tyne, east of Newcastle.

2./JG 27 pilots playing cards at Leeuwarden airfield in the Netherlands in March/April 1943. Standing at left is Fw Hahnrieder, centre is Lt Karl Wünsch and on his left is Uffz Ernst Nickammer.

Bf 109 G-4 "Black 6" of 2./JG 27 being serviced at Leeuwarden in early spring 1943. This squadron was assigned to the defence of the Reich for a short period, as at the end of May it was transferred to Marignane in the south of France.

Right and below: One of the first
Bf 109 G-6s delivered to I./JG 3 at
Mönchengladbach in May 1943, this 2.
Staffel plane, like that of 3. Staffel behind it,
is armed with 20mm cannons.

Above left: The new Kommodore of JG 1, Major Hans Philipp, having claimed his 205th kill on May 16th, 1943. Promoted to Obstlt, he was shot down on the following October 8th whilst adding a B-17 to his scoresheet.

Above right: The increasing presence of Eighth Air Force heavy bombers in the skies over Europe compelled the Luftwaffe to form, in mid-1943, special units charged with testing new materials and techniques specifically developed to combat the B-17s and B-24s. One of these was JG 50, directed by Major Hermann Graf, reportedly the first man in the world to achieve 200 aerial victories.

Below left: Reichsmarschall Herman Göring and his chief of staff Generaloberst Hans Jeschonnek, photographed at Klessheim Castle (near Berghof, in the Salzburg region) in April 1943. After having mistakenly ordered a flak battery to fire on Luftwaffe planes during the Allied bombing of Peenemünde on the night of August 17th/18th, 1943, Jeschonnek committed suicide in Hitler's headquarters at Rustenburg.

Below right: Jeschonnek's replacement as Chef des Generalstab d.Lw. was Gen dFl. Günther Korten. Seriously wounded on July 20th, 1944 during the bomb attack against Hitler, he died two days later.

Former technical officer of III./JG 26, Hptm Rolf Schrödter, became commander of a small test unit based at Heiligenbeil, East Prussia, in the summer of 1943, which is where this long-distance FW 190 A-5/U8 fighter-bomber was photographed. The supplementary 300-litre tanks are attached under the wings; in later versions (FW 190 G-2s, G-3s and G-8s) the attachment structures were more streamlined.

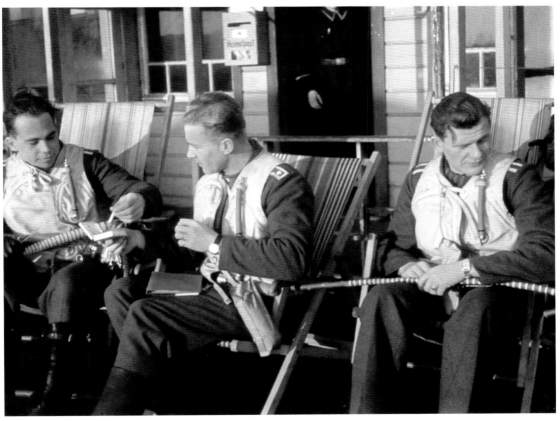

This photograph of three unidentified fighter pilots was probably taken on the Western Front in 1943, The "kill stick" of the man on the left is marked with at least 22 notches, representing his aerial victories; the man on the right has at least 37 notches on his.

Some of the commanders of German night defence operatiosn meet during the spring of 1943 at Erprobungsstelle d.Lw. Werneuchen, a test centre 30km north-east of Berlin. From left is Obstlt Wolfgang Falck (commander of NJG 1), GenLt Wolfgang Martini (chief of radar communications), GenOb Hans-Jürgen Stumpff (commander of Luftflotte 5) and GenMaj Andreas Nielsen (chief of staff of Luftflotte 5).

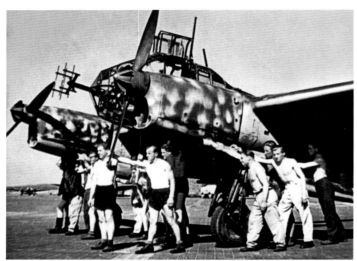

To tackle the small Soviet biplanes that harassed German troops at night, the twin-engined observation FW 189 was converted into an improvised night fighter with a single-antenna FuG 212 Lichtenstein radar, an MG 150/20 cannon with oblique shooting at the rear and a flame suppressor on the exhaust. Here the prototype is being tested at Werneuchen during the summer of 1943. Thirty of these planes were produced and used during March 1945 by NJG 5 and NJG 100.

Another plane modified for night fighting at Werneuchen in the autumn of 1943 was Messerschmitt Bf 109 G-6 PP+WO (W.Nr. 160811), whose FuG 217 Neptun J-1 radar is here being calibrated.

Hptm Manfred Meurer, Staffelkapitän of 3./NJG 1, wearing the Knight's Cross with oak leaves he was awarded on August 2nd, 1943. This great Nachtjagd ace registered 65 victories before his He 219 A-0 crashed into an RAF Avro Lancaster bomber over Magdeburg, on the night of January 21st/22nd, 1944.

One of the stranger prototypes tested at Werneuchen, this Ju 88 P-2 tank fighter was transformed into a night fighter with an FuG 212 radar in its nose and two Mk 103 30mm cannons in an enormous F1-A-103Z underbelly gondola. In front of this are the "organ pipes" that allow aircraft returning from missions to be identified as "friends". This plane's performance was so poor that testing was stopped almost as soon as it began.

This Lockheed P-38G T9+XB, photographed at the Rechlin test centre on September 19th, 1943, belonged to Sonderkommando Rosarius, nicknamed "the Circus", the test unit for Allied materials in 2./Versuchsverband Oberbefehlshaber. Though this plane's exact identity remains unknown, it is thought to be a Fifteenth Air Force Lightning, captured on the Mediterranean Front and brought back to Berlin by Fw Heinz Girnth of 9./JG 53. Its engines were damaged by poor-octane gasoline and the plane never flew again. Its code was re-assigned to a Mosquito B Mk IV in 1944.

Left: Three of the best German bomber pilots of the Second World War photographed on January 20th, 1944, during a medal ceremony at Hitler's HQ in Rastenburg (the famous Wolf's Lair). From left: Obstlt Joachim Helbig, Kommodore of LG 1, GenMaj Dietrich Peltz, commander-in-chief of IX. Fliegerkorps, and Maj Werner Baumbach, inspector of bombing aviation.

Above: Obstlt Alfred Helm, joint commander of the Truppenversuchskommando of Werneuchen, in front of Bf 110 G-4 _R+TQ equipped with an FuG 220 Lichtenstein SN-2c radar, in the spring of 1944. At 50, Helm was the oldest night fighter pilot in the Luftwaffe. This former spotter in the Great War – in the course of which he reported three victories in KG 5/Kasta 30 – joined the Nachtjagd in 1941. Detached several times to operational units, he added two Halifaxes and a Wellington to his scoresheet between June and August 1942.

Far left: Major Berhard Jope, Kommodore of the KG 100, received the Knight's Cross with oak leaves on 24th March 1944.

Left: Walter Krupinski, who has just received the Knight's Cross with oak leaves. Transferred from JG 5 to JG 11 and then JG 6, this ace ended the war flying an Me 262 in JV 44 with a tally of 197 kills.

This page features a heavy flak battery on the Western Front. The stereoscopic Kommandogerät 36 range-finder, which controlled the firing of the Flak 18 88mm gun, is particularly interesting as it was rarely photographed. In the image on the bottom left, a corporal is holding an 88mm shell.

On April 25th, 1944, Schwäbisch-Hall, 50km north-east of Stuttgart, was hit by Allied bombers which destroyed six He 177 A-3s of IV./KG 100 and damaged four others. Engines turning, one of the bombers taxies onto the runway to escape the blaze; in the hangar on the left is 6N+HU of 10. Staffel.

The Blohm & Voss 222 V7 TB+QL (W.Nr. 310007) photographed on two different occasions in 1944 on Lake Schaal in Schleswig-Holstein. The prototype of the marine version of the BV 222 C with diesel Jumo 207 C in-line engines, this Wiking became the X4+FH. It was scuttled on May 3rd, 1945 off Travemünde.

A 20mm anti-aircraft cannon in position on the English Channel. Luftwaffe flak units were among the first to intervene when Allied troops began landing in Normandy in the early hours of June 6th, 1944.

The crew of He 177 A-3 6N+HK (W.Nr. 332235) of 2./KG 100 pose in a Volkswagen Kübelwagen at Châteaudun in March 1944. The bombers of this group were engaged in Operation *Steinbock*, a series of night attacks on British towns. This plane, named *Helga*, was destroyed at Cloyes-sur-le-Loire on April 27th, returning from a raid on Portsmouth.

Luftwaffe heroes are received by the Führer on April 4th, 1944 at his Alpine residence of Berghof, near Berchtesgaden. From left: Maj Werner Streib, commander of NJG 1; Hptm Gerhard Barkhorn, commander of II./JG 52; Oberst Erich Walther, commander of Fallschirmjäger-Regiment 4; Maj Kurt Bühligen, commander of II./JG 2; Hptm Hans-Joachim Jabs, commander of IV./NJG 1; Maj Bernhard Jope, commander of KG 100; Maj Reinhard Seiler, commander of I./JG 54; Maj Hans-Georg Bätcher, commander of I./KG 4 (masked behind Hitler); Hptm Horst Ademeit, commander of I./JG 54; Maj Johannes Weise, commander of I./JG 52; Wachtsmeister Fritz Petersen, commander of the 6th Battery Flak-Regiment 4; Maj Dr Maximillian Otte, commander of II./SG 2; and Oblt Walter Krupinski, commander of 7./JG 52. Absent is Lt Erich Hartmann, commander of 9./JG 52.

The front of a Junkers 290 A-5 equipped with an FuG 200 Hohentwiel radar for finding convoys at sea. Only a few dozen of these four-engined planes (derived from the Ju 90 civil transport) were built from the end of 1942. This type of plane, benefitting from a superior range of 6,000km, was mostly used before 1944 by I./Fernaufklärungsgruppe 5 (FAGr 5), a maritime long-range reconnaissance group operating from the Mont-de-Marsan base south of Bordeaux.

Right: Lt Adolf "Addi" Glunz, commander of 6./JG 26, is one of the Jagdwaffe *experten* who made an impression during the Normandy landings. He received the oak leaves to his Knight's Cross on June 24th, 1944 after his 65th kill.

Left: Official portrait of Oblt Emil Lang, Staka 9./JG 54, taken just after he was decorated with the oak leaves to his Knight's Cross in April 1944 for his 144th victory. On the older end of the fighter pilot spectrum (35 years old), "Bully" Lang claimed 28 kills between June 8th and August 26th, 1944, confirming his status as the greatest ace on the Normandy front. However, his talents were not enough to save him in the face of the superior Allied air power, and he was shot down and killed by P-51 Mustangs on September 3rd.

The wreck of a Ju 88 A hit by Allied flak at Martragny, south-east of Bayeux, Normandy, on July 17th, 1944.

With the activities of the French Resistance intensifying in the centre of the country, a small anti-partisan unit was created in April 1944 under the name of Geschwader Bongart, from the name of its head, Obstlt Hermann-Josef Freiherr von dem Bongart. The unit used many types of planes, the most common being the Italian Reggiane 2002, such as this Re 2002 "Black 2" (BN+YB) abandoned at Bron. Based at Lyon-Bron, Bourges, Clermont-Ferrand and Avord, the Geschwader Bongart was particularly active during July in the repression of the uprising at Vercors. The unit was disbanded on September 4th, 1944 at Luxeuil.

American aviators pose on an FW 190 A–8 abandoned at Reims-Champagne. This region was occupied by II./JG 6 and I./JG 11 until its liberation at the end of August 1944.

This series of photographs was taken on the Villacoublay/Süd base during autumn 1944.

The repair and assembly workshops in the foreground were used from March 1942 by the Junkers firm, who established the Frontreparaturbetrieb GL 2561 here. Though the majority of planes were Ju 88 A bombers, in one of the photographs is a Ju 88 G-1 night fighter with pale grey camouflage. The last two photographs show some French twin-engined Lioré and Olivier LeO 451Ts, converted into transport planes with their under surfaces painted yellow. Most of the planes here were probably damaged during the bombing raid by B-17s of the Eighth Air Force on August 11th, 1944. The base was evacuated by the Germans 11 days later, just before it was liberated by the French 2nd Armoured Division of General Leclerc. After that, American specialists of the 818th Engineer Aviation Battalion demined and swept the area, removed the wrecks, and turned it into an operational base for the USAAF. *(Philippe Ricco collection)*

The high-altitude Gustav fighters of II./JG 27 seen in July/August 1944 on the slopes of Fels am Wagram, Austria, from where the group defended Vienna. In the foreground, with its landing gear painted red (to advise mechanics that this plane has an MW-50 overpower device and must therefore receive C3 100 octane fuel), is Bf 109 G-6/ASy "Yellow 2" (W.Nr. 412807) of 6. Staffel, which was shot down at Loosdorf on August 23rd. Behind it, Bf 109 G-6/AS "White 5" (W.Nr. 413918) of 5. Staffel, was shot down by an Allied fighter on August 16th, 13km north-east of Holzminden.

Far left: A great ace in the *zerstörer*, or destroyer, mould, with 16 daytime victories, Hans-Joachim Jabs transferred to the Nachtjagd where he continued to add to his scoresheet. This photo was taken during the summer of 1944, when he, as a major, commanded NJG 1. He survived the war with a tally of 50 kills, 30 of which were obtained at night.

Left: Promoted to commander of Luftflotte 3 on August 22nd, 1944, Generaloberst Otto Dessloch subsequently organized the bombing of the American columns pushing towards Paris. The raid, carried out on the night of August 26th/27th, killed numerous civilians in and around the French capital.

Bottom: Another victim of the fighting of August 16th, 1944, Bf 109 G-6 AS "White 9" (W.Nr. 412556) of 7./JG 27, shot down in the Issingenhausen area.

The Normandy landings didn't stop the Allied raids on Greater Germany. Shot down in combat on June 27th, 1944 around Budapest, Me 410 B-2 "Black M8+7" (W.Nr. 150124) of 5./ZG 76 crashed in a maize field near Fölsöls, Hungary. The red Reich-defence band and yellow panels are clearly visible on the undersides of the wings.

Intended as a replacement for the Bf 110 and Ju 88 night fighters, the Heinkel 219 Uhu only numbered 250 units as its performance was barely superior to that of its predecessors. Most of these were engaged in operations by I./NJG 1, who used it with great success until the end of the war, The W.Nr. 290213 visible here is one of the first He 219 A-2s built by the Heinkel factory at Rostock-Marienehe in July 1944.

The tenth specimen of a pre-series B-0 of the Arado 234 twinjet, Ar 234 S-10 E2+20 (W.Nr. 140110), was acquired by the Erprobungstelle at Rechlin on August 10th, 1944. It was used the following November to test the FuG 203 radio system that would later guide the Henschel 293 anti-ship missile.

Me 262 V303 (W.Nr. 170303), second V7 prototype, at Lechfeld during summer 1944. This Schwalbe is equipped with an experimental wooden stabilizer.

A close-up of the nose of Messerschmitt Me 262 A-1a KL+WJ (W.Nr. 170056), which was turned into the second V2 prototype so it could be used to test the FuG 218 and 226 radar systems. After being involved in an accident on December 12th, 1944, this plane was captured by the Americans on April 29th, 1945.

Photographed in July 1944 at the Silesian airfield of Sagan–Küpper, this Supermarine Spitfire PR.XI of the Zirkus Rosarius is often identified as T9+BB, serial MB945 of 14.PRS/7.PRG of the USAAF, captured on March 1st, 1944. It is, in reality, T9+EK ex-serial EN685 of 542 Squadron RAF, forced to land near Hanover on May 13th, 1944. This reconnaissance Spitfire was kept on in the Luftwaffe as "Blue PRU" with its lower surfaces and tail repainted yellow.

An array of II./KG 100's Heinkel 177 As at the Aalborg-West airfield in the summer of 1944.

This Junkers Ju 88 G-1 night fighter, with its unique identification letter A on its nose, was photographed at Grove, Denmark, during autumn 1944. It is equipped with an FuG 220 Lichtenstein SN-2c radar – the characteristic antennae of this device are hard to miss.

Above: Heinz Schnaufer (centre) with his crew after receiving the Knight's Cross with swords and diamonds on November 21st, 1944, in Berlin. On the left is Lt Fritz Rumpelhardt (radar operator) and Ofw Wilhelm Gansler (machine-gunner) is on the right. Schnaufer, who was at this time of Kommodore NJG 4, was the second night fighter pilot to receive this decoration after Obstlt Helmut Lent who was killed a few weeks earlier.

Right: Despite an increasingly desperate military situation, the German high command believed that a miraculous change in their fortunes was possible. From left: Generalfeldmarschall Wilhelm Keitel, Reichsmarschall Hermann Göring, Grossadmiral Karl Dönitz, Reichsführer SS Heinrich Himmler, and the Führer's personal secretary, Martin Bormann. All were later found guilty of war crimes by the Allies, but only Göring, Keitel and Dönitz were tried at Nuremberg as Himmler and Bormann had already disappeared. Keitel was hanged and Dönitz sentenced to ten years in prison, but the former head of the Luftwaffe poisoned himself before he could be executed.

Above and left: On January 1st, 1945, in delayed (because of the poor weather) support of the Wehrmacht, which was losing the Ardennes Offensive, Luftwaffe fighters attempted last-minute raids on grounded Allied aircraft. Operation *Bodenplatte* resulted in failure, with hugely disproportionate human losses for the Germans, though material losses in the two camps were similar. These two photographs show FW 190 A-8/R2 "White 11" (W.Nr. 681 497) of 5.(Sturm)/JG 4, with its pilot standing alongside it, at Saint-Trond after having been hit by anti-aircraft fire. The aviators of 404th Fighter Group later managed to restore the plane in order to test it.

Left: Formerly the commander of JG 54, Oberst Hannes Trautloft (53 kills, plus five in Spain), became the inspector of day fighters in December 1943. Disgraced after the famous "Kommodore Revolt" against Göring, following the disastrous Operation *Bodenplatte*, Trautloft ended the war as head of 4. Fliegerschule Division.

Part XIII

Second Line
and Training Units

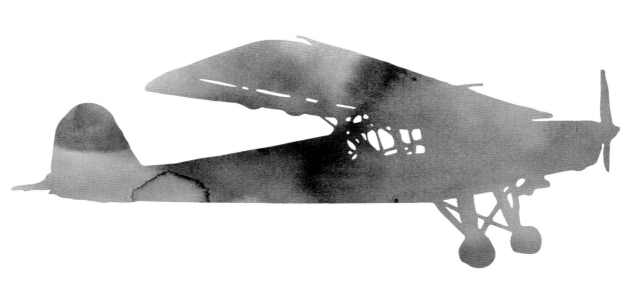

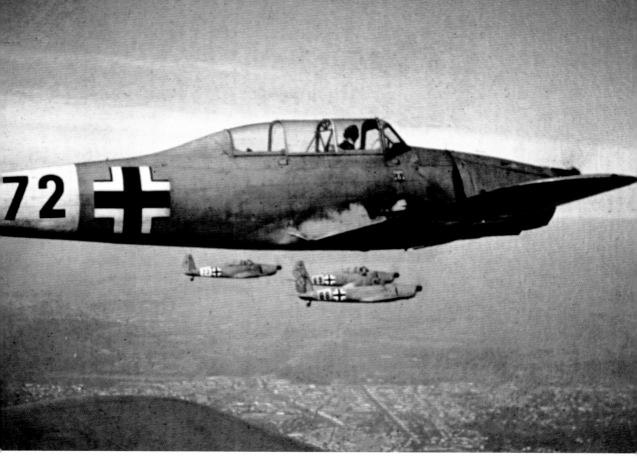

Above: During the latter part of the war, the Luftwaffe was forced onto the defensive, and to train increasingly higher numbers of fighter pilots. The workhorse of this training programme was the excellent twin-engined Arado 96, several examples of which are seen here flying over Paris in February 1942. Ar 96 Bs 69, 72, 73 and 88 belong to Jagdfliegerschule 5 based at Villacoublay.

Left: Like the majority of training planes, Caudron C.445 DS+KP (no. 9026/298) has an entirely yellow underside. This plane belonged to Flugzeugführerschule A/B 118 based at Stettin-Altdamm on the Baltic coast.

3./JFS 5 student pilots have a snack before beginning their practical training.

Airmen gather on the Toussus-le-Noble satellite airfield. The supervisor wearing the flying cap is Oblt Harald von Arnim.

Harald von Arnim checking on his students in the skies of France. The Staffelkapitän looks happy with their performance.

Top left: Arado 96 B 70 in formation. The plane is painted in grey-green RLM 02, except for the yellow band on the fuselage which shows it is a training plane.

Left: Relegated to training status, this Messerschmitt 109 – a Bf 109 D-1 Dora – is an older version of the previous Bf 109 E.

Below: 3./JFS 5 instructors playing cards by an open fire, under the watchful eye of Göring's portrait.

A BV 138 C-1 seaplane during a testing session at the Blohm & Voss factory in Hamburg in April/May 1942. This three-engined aircraft was probably part of the PG+KA to PG+KT series (W.Nr. 10101 to 10120).

An FW 189 Uhu fresh from the factory. This small twin-engined observation twin-boom replaced the Hs 126s in the Auflklärungstaffel operating on the Eastern Front in the spring of 1942.

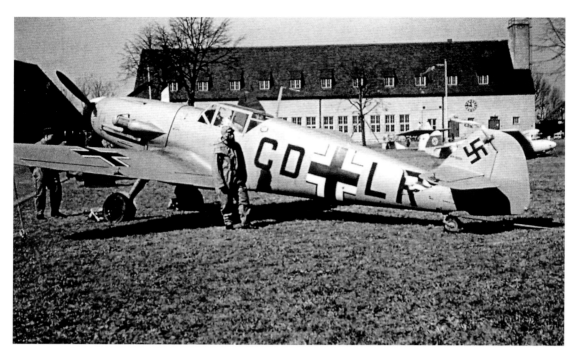

Coming out of the Erla Leipzig factory in March 1942, Bf 109 F-4 CD+LR (W.Nr. 10124) joined II./JG 5, where it was severely damaged (55%) when landing at Petsamo on July 2nd, 1942. Repaired, it was transferred to the flight school seen here. The planes in the background are Göppingen 3 Minimoa gliders.

On his retirement from the front in February 1943, where he had carried out resupply missions at Stalingrad, Oblt Herbert Kuntz was named the head of 10./KG 100 training squadron. Here he is at the controls of a Heinkel 111 at Schwäbisch-Hall, wearing the Knight's Cross he received on March 14th, 1943 in recognition of his 365 combat missions, during which he sank 16 ships and damaged 11 others. He ended the war as a Mistel flying-bomb pilot in 6./KG 200.

Right:
Manufacturing
Bf 110 rudders at
the Messerschmitt
factory.

Left and above: A production line of Messerschmitt Bf 109 G-6s at the Erla factory in Leipzig-Mockau in October 1943. The fuselages are pale blue while the tails appear to be beige. These fighters belong to the lot bearing the factory numbers 31132069 to 31132100, which became W.Nrs 410672 to W.Nr. 410703. (Signal)

Three views of Focke-Wulf 190s of JG 104, based at Fürth, near Nuremberg, in the spring of 1943. Behind "Blue 4" (W.Nr. 20235) can be seen a Bf 109 E and a row of Ar 96s, as well as an FW 190 A-2, which was sent to the Auxerre repair workshop in September; it did not re-emerge until February 1944. The planes still carry the insignia of the Jagdfliegerschule 4, which was succeeded by the Jagdgeschwader 104 in March 1943.

Left: Flight schools gratefully welcomed all kinds of old planes into their training fleets, such as this Junkers 87 A "Anton" of the Stukaschule Saint-Raphäel (IV./StG 101), seen in flight over the Côte d'Azur in mid–1943.

Right: A cement bomb being hung from the belly of a Ju 87 B-1 of the Stukaschule Saint-Raphäel in early summer 1943. The base was abandoned by the Luftwaffe and rendered unusable by autumn 1943.

Below: Student pilot Hans-Georg Kister poses next to Bü 131 DB+FN (W.Nr. 419x) of the Oschatz-based FFS A 61, on February 2nd, 1944. The school's emblem, twin towers surmounted by a rampant lion, is on the cowling.

Right: An instructor explains an attacking manoeuvre to two of his students. The Bf 109 is an old pressurized G-1 (note the pellets at the bottom of the glass canopy) that has been converted to a G–2 – as shown by the absence of the vertical plate that ensured the airtightness of the rear cabin.

Below: Flights had to continue, even in winter, as shown in this photo of Arado Ar 96 B "Orange 338" on a recently snow-cleared runway.

This photograph is interesting as it shows FW 190 F–3s of Umrüstaffel I./SG 152 stationed at Prossnitz in early spring 1944. The planes carry the unit code 4M+_F, but no individual identification letters are visible.

The Luftwaffe wasn't just made up of pilots, navigators and mechanics. Other than the anti-aircraft artillery already mentioned, the air force brought together a wide range of skills and specialists, the most diverse of which formed the Luftnachrichten, or transmission corps.

Luftwaffe transmissions personnel unit pose outside their barracks at Köthen – between Leipzig and Magdeburg – on August 8th, 1944. They are probably from the Stab/Ln.-Versuchs-Rgt or the Peilfluger-Lehrgänge Köthen.

A transmissions *unteroffizier* (sergeant), identified by his brown collar panels.

This *oberfeldwebel* (staff sergeant) is also part of the Luftnachrichten.

A meteorologist prepares to launch a weather balloon.

Examining aerial photos.

Above and left: Installation of a radio communications post.

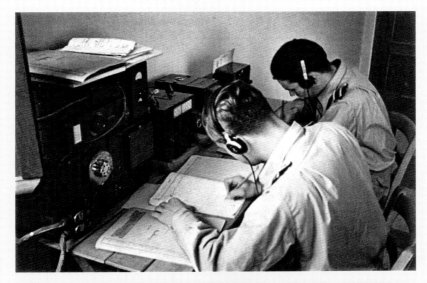

Transmissions officers working at their posts.

Cartographers at work.

"Soup's up!" – a moment enjoyed by armed forces the world over.

Right: Still draped in camouflage netting, FW 190 F-2 "Blue 16" of JG 103 is seen here in Copenhagen-Kastrup at the end of the war.

Above: This Siebel Si 204 D-1 "White 1" captured by American forces in Germany is probably KL+QD (W.Nr. 321498). It has the two yellow bands indicative of an instrument flight training school (*Blindflugschule*).

Right: The wreckage of Bf 109 G-6 "Black 479" of 4./JG 104 photographed at Fürth in May/June 1945.

Bottom right: Another plane captured at Fürth: Siebel Si 204 D-1 KJ+RN (W.Nr. 241523?) of FFS B 3 instrument flight training school.

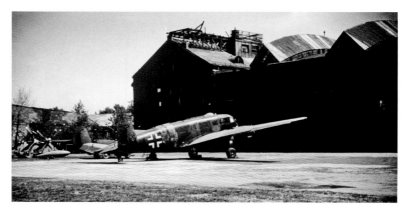

Part XIV

The Eagle Falls

This Bf 109 G–14 "Yellow 5" of 3./JG 53 was discovered in early April 1945 by troops of the American 80th Division in the grounds of the Henschel factory at Kassel. *(NARA)*

Me 262 A–1a/U3 (W.Nr. 170111) of Kommando Braunegg had a disastrous landing at Schwäbisch–Hall after its port engine failed on January 1st, 1945; the unit commander, Oblt Herward Braunegg, was himself at the controls. Luckily, the plane was only 5% damaged, and was soon repaired and transferred to 2./NAGr 6, where it became "White 26".

Messerschmitt Me 262 A-1a "White 13" of III./EJG 2 at Lechfeld, February 1945. Formed in November 1944 from Erprobungskommando 262, III./Ergänzungs-Jagdgeschwader 2 was disbanded on April 27th, 1945 and absorbed into GenMaj Adolf Galland's renowned Jagdverband 44.

Me 262 A-1a "White 17" (W.Nr. 110956) of 10./EJG 2, captured at Lechfeld on April 29th, 1945. This plane was acquired by Fw Franz Holzinger and reserved for training, as indicated by the letter S (for Schule) on the fuselage and the tailfin.

When the hunter becomes the hunted ... photographed in the Vechta region near Osnabrück during the summer of 1945, this wreck was once Ju 88 G-6 4R+PP (W.Nr. 621126) of 6./NJG 2, destroyed the previous January.

An SdKfz 7/1 caterpillar armed with a Flakvierling 38 at Fischhausen, East Prussia, in March 1945.

Powered by two DB 603 A-2s with a combined 3,500hp, the twin-tandem Dornier 335 A achieved a speed of 732kph at 7,100m. But only a few dozen of these large single-seater Zerstörer were ever built, and only a handful actually entered service before the end of the war. This one is the fifth A-0 destroyer of the series, W.Nr. 240105 (VG+IK), acquired by Erkdo 335 and captured by American troops in April 1945 at the Dornier factory in Oberpfaffenhofen, Bavaria. *(Philippe Ricco collection)*

An anti-aircraft gun team mans a 20mm Flak 30 cannon on a rooftop.

Some of the planes captured at Langensalza (30km north-west of Erfurt) on April 7th, 1945. Alongside the Ju 88 G-6 night fighter is FW 190 D-9 "White 12" (W.Nr. 500408) of 5./JG 301. *(Philippe Ricco collection)*

Left: Top JG 2 and then JG 54 ace, Maj Erich Rudorffer, took the lead in I./JG 7 in his Me 262. He shot down 12 Allied planes in his jet, which, by the end of the war, was adorned with a bar for each of his 219 wartime kills.

Right: On January 1st, 1945, Major Hans-Ulrich Rudel, Kommodore of SG 2, became the only Luftwaffe pilot to receive the Knight's Cross with golden oak leaves, swords and diamonds. Shot down by Soviet flak the following February 9th, he returned to combat despite having his right leg amputated, and ended the war flying a Ju 87 G-2 with the prodigious score of 519 tanks destroyed in 2,530 war missions – a world record. This did not take into account the bridges, vehicles and armoured trains he destroyed.

The results of a bombing raid by B-17s of the Eighth Air Force on the Dornier factory on April 9th, 1945. In the foreground is the unfinished fuselage of a Do 335. *(NARA)*

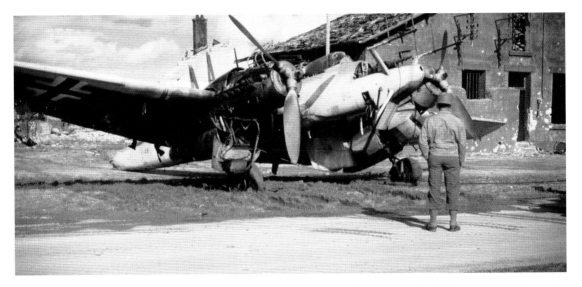

The wreck of a Bf 110 G-4 night fighter with the C9 code of NJG 5 on its fuselage. To facilitate the identification of planes by anti-aircraft batteries, the underside of the right wing was painted black.

A Mistel 1 of II./KG 200 prepares to enter the fray on the runway at Burg in April 1945. The guide-plane, a Bf-109 F-4, is numbered 39 – painted on at a repairs workshop (*reparatur-werkstatt*) – while the "flying bomb" is Ju 88 A-4 "Red 6" (W.Nr. 5757), seen previously in Part X (Face to Face with the Soviet Steamroller) in mid-1942 on the Crimean steppes. Behind the composite "Beethoven" is a Mistel 2, made up of an FW 190 A-8 or F-8 and a Ju 88 G-1.

Hptm Herbert Kuntz of 6./KG 200 takes off from Burg in a Beethoven for a training sortie in early April 1945. He is piloting a Mistel 2 that is not armed with the usual 3.5-ton explosive charge in its nose.

Two Me 163s destroyed by German troops retreating from Polenz, a satellite airfield at Brandis where I./JG was based, in March 1945.

Close-up of another scuttled Me 163 that bears the insignia of 13./JG 400, one of the Komet training squadrons, Die Schwarze 13 (The Black 13).

The Brunswick–Waggum airfield in Lower Saxony was captured on April 12th, 1945 by the Ninth US Army, who discovered a diverse range of planes. Amongst them, Ju 88 G-6 4R+FB of Stab I./NJG 2 stands on the right alongside a Ju 188 and two FW 190s.

Abandoned aircraft at Halberstadt near Magdeburg, Saxony. In the foreground, FW 190 A-9 "Yellow 8" (W.Nr. 206147?) of 7./JG 301 has an unusual horizontal bar on its rear fuselage, like all the Jagdgeschwader 301 groups. Behind it is Bf 109 G-14/AS "Yellow 8", which probably belonged to 6./JG 27, and, on the left, two Gotha 242 gliders coded DQ+AW and DY+BI (or SN+BI).

Above: A line-up of Bücker 181s at Bøtø, on the Danish island of Falster, in May 1945. While the first of these planes was a training plane, those with fuselage crosses painted over in black are from Nachtschlachtkommando 1 of Warnemünde. They have been modified to carry two Panzerfaust rocket launchers on their wings, with which they would – in theory – be able to destroy Allied armoured vehicles.

Below: A close-up of Ju 52/3m MS 3K+GH of Minensuchgruppe 1, abandoned in May 1945 at Bøtø-Falster. The Duralumin ring used to detonate mines by means of a magnetic field has already been dismantled, as has the rudder.

Operating in the Baltic in the spring of 945, Dornier 24 T-3 seaplanes of the Seenotgruppe 81 took refuge in the bay of Guldborg, Denmark, on May 4th, to escape the advancing Soviet forces. They returned to Germany on June 18th, carrying wounded soldiers and interned German civilians, escorted by Hawker Typhoons from 175 and 184 Squadrons of the RAF.

A stunning shot of a Ju 188 E-1 with near-indiscernible identification markings outside a hangar camouflaged as a Scandinavian farmstead. The camouflage corresponds to that applied to the Junkers of I./KG 66, as confirmed by the virtually invisible Z6 on the tailfin. This bomber group ended the war at Stavanger-Sola, in the south-west of Norway.

Above: A former Danish airport, Copenhagen-Kastrup harboured many Luftwaffe night fighter groups from 1943 to 1945, and is seen here in May 1945 with RAF Hawker Typhoons in the background, and Ju 88 G-1 D9+PH (W.Nr. 712344) of 1./NJG 7 alongside Bf 109 G-14 "White 11" of an unidentified unit in the foreground. *(DR)*

Right: Two soldiers admiring the front of a Junkers 88 G-6 of 4./NJG 3, designated Nachtjagdstaffel Norwegen until March 1st, 1945.

Above: Left in the open for several weeks outside the Messerschmitt factory in Augsburg, the wreck of Bf 109 G-14 W.Nr. 165545 has started to rust. This single-seater, intended for use in test flights, crashed when leaving for its posting at Memmingen. *(NARA)*

Below: The remains of two Me 410 heavy fighters in the Messerschmitt factory at Augsburg.

Photographed at Kastrup in May 1945, Ju 88 R–q 7J+QK (W.Nr. 751066) is a former night fighter of 2./NJG 102. The wings and front of this plane have been painted a mottled camouflage, while the back of the fuselage and the tail still have a two-toned green camouflage pattern. The Englandblitz insignia (left) was always painted on the Ju 88 C–6s of NJG 3.

Also seen at Copenhagen–Kastrup at the end of the war, this Ju 88 C-6 belongs to I./NJG 3. Note that the underbelly gondola has been removed – a modification that added 30 kph to the plane's top-end speed.

Two Ju-88 G-6s and a Bf 110 G-4 are inspected by GIs at the Neubiberg aerodrome, 8km south-east of Munich, in April 1945. These planes appear to have belonged to IV./NJG 6 that operated from Neubiberg using these two types of night fighter.

An Me 410 fighter jet found hidden on the side of the Munich–Salzburg motorway, at Brunnthal. The plane, vulnerable against the Allied fighters, belonged to a unit that had been disbanded. By May 1945, only one squadron still used this plane in a zerstörer role: 11./ZG 26, based in Norway. *(NARA)*

This Me 410, also found at Brunnthal at the end of April 1945, is B-2/U4, with the factory code BW+HQ (W.Nr. 710458). Note the impressive armament on this aircraft: a 50mm BK 5 cannon in the nose, intended for use against Allied bombers. *(NARA)*

Patrolling south-east of Munich at the end of April 1945, these American soldiers have just discovered a Schwalbe, on the edge of the Hofoldinger forest at Brunnthal. Me 262 A-2a 9K+FH (W.Nr. 111685) is an old fighter-bomber of 1./KG 51, which had recently been donated to JV 44. It has been stripped of its engines and the four 30mm nose cannons. *(NARA)*

When soldiers of the American 16th Armored Division arrived at the Pilsen base in western Czechoslovakia on May 6th, 1945, they found a perfectly intact Ju 87 G-2. This version of the Stuka, here equipped with a flame suppressor for nighttime operations, was specially developed for anti-tank operations: it was armed with a pair of Flak 18 37mm cannons under its wings. *(NARA)*

JV44's junkyard: in the centre is the tailplane of an Me 262, and on the right, in front of a red and white FW 190 Long-Nose, the front of a Heinkel He 162 Volksjäger. *(Philippe Ricco collection)*

More than 230 Savoia S.82s were in service in the Luftwaffe by June 30th, 1944. Like this "Red A" abandoned on the edge of an airfield now occupied by Republic P-47D Thunderbolts, these large three-engined transports served until the German capitulation.

He 111 W.Nr. 701152 A3+HL (NT+SL) of KG 200 was also recovered in the Munich area, this time by aviators of the famous 56th Fighter Group. Transferred to the British after having been painted black and recoded HV-C, the Heinkel carried out a forced landing at Farnborough on May 5th, 1945. This plane is the H–20 type (not the H–23 type as is often claimed), modified to drop paratroops, and can still be seen at the RAF Museum, Hendon. *(56th FG)*

These film shots show FW 190 F-8 "Green <2" (W.Nr. 568875) of II./SG 10 en route to US forces at Neubiberg on May 8th, 1945. This fighter-bomber, like FW 190 A-8 "Yellow 8" in the third photograph, bears the markings of an Eastern Front reconnaissance unit.

To protect the Me 262s of his JV 44, very vulnerable on take-off and landing, General Adolf Galland created an aerodrome protection squadron (Platzschutzstaffel), which was equipped with Focke-Wulf 190 "Long-Noses". These FW 190 D-9s and D11s had their undersides painted bright red with thin white stripes to make them easily identifiable to flak batteries at Munich-Riem. *(Philippe Ricco collection)*

FW 189 A-2 5H+RK of 2./NAGr 16 took refuge at Salzburg to escape the Soviets. This end-of-series plane, with twin 7.92mm MG 81 Z guns in its turret, had yellow tailfins and a 50cm yellow band over its engine cowlings; these tactical reconnaissance markings were adopted by IV. Fliegerkorps on March 7th, 1945.

Above: Wels aerodrome, south-west of Linz, remained until early May 1945 one of the last operational Luftwaffe airfields in Austria. These two Messerschmitt Bf 109s, the yellow-banded G-14 and the precariously angled G-6, are probably from Ergänzungskampfgeschwader (Jagd) – or Erg.KG(J) – a unit intended to convert former bomber pilots of IV./KG 27 and IV./KG 55 into fighter pilots, but which was disbanded in November 1944.

Right: As surrenders began to multiply in the West and the Mediterranean, German airmen on the Eastern Front decided to fight until the last possible moment. Major Erich Hartmann, commander of I./JG 52, claimed his 352nd – and last – kill, a Yak-9, on May 8th, 1945, just before surrendering to the American forces who, 16 days later, delivered him to the Soviets. He wasn't released until 1955.

Like the USAAF, the Luftwaffe used Liberators in its operations, albeit in much reduced numbers. This B-24H-5-DT (s/n 41-28641) of 735th Bomber Squadron, 453rd Bomber Group was lost during a training sortie on February 4th, 1944; hit by flak, it was captured near Eger in Czechoslovakia. Repaired and given the code (A3)+KB. It was incorporated into KG 200 – the famous special mission squadron – where it served at the end of 1944, resupplying the island of Rhodes. It is seen here after its "liberation" by the Americans in Salzburg in May 1945. The four-engined plane, whose underside has been painted yellow, was abandoned after having broken its front undercarriage strut during a rough landing.

Above: Messerschmitt Bf 109 K-4s abandoned in a hangar at Nuremberg at the end of April 1945.

Left: Reichsmarschall Hermann Göring in full dress uniform. Renounced by Hitler just before he committed suicide on April 30th, 1945, the former head of the Luftwaffe surrendered to American troops on May 7th. He spent his final days on trial at Nuremberg but killed himself on October 15th, 1946 before he could be executed.

Above: Like his Messerschmitt colleagues, the pilot of FW 190 D-9 "Blue 12" (W.Nr. 500570) of II./JG 6 chose to surrender to the American troops surrounding the Fürth aerodrome.

Left: In front of Bf 109 G-10/R2 of Nahaufklärungsgruppe 14 and P-51D of the 10th PRG, the Focke-Wulf 190 Red 5 is this time the A-8 type.

Below: Three Stukas of 2./NSGr 10, equipped with flame suppressors, land at Fürth on the last day of the war. Among them is Junkers 87 D-5N 5B+LK (W.Nr. 141286).

On May 8th, 1945, Fürth airfield, situated just west of Nuremberg, welcomed a number of German air units seeking refuge from the Eastern Front. Bf 109 G-10/R2 Black 5F+12 (W.Nr. 770269) is a 2./NAG 14 single-seater tactical reconnaissance plane whose doors have here been removed. Behind it, just visible, is P-51D-10-NA Mustang s/n 44–14082 Skipper of the 10th Photo Recon Group (10th PRG).

Above: Two views of Bf 109 K-4 "White 8" on its belly behind US lines on May 8th, 1945. The plane, which very likely belonged to I./JG 52, has the "end of the war" dark green and red-brown camouflage on its upper surfaces.

Bf 109 G-10/U4 "Yellow 3", captured at the same time, has a classic camouflage pattern: dark green and medium grey, with speckles on the flanks of its fuselage. The war in the West was over, and with it the Third Reich's dreams of grandeur. The majority of the planes shown in this final chapter were ruthlessly broken up, and the scrap metal produced allowed Europe to begin rebuilding …